DEATH BY DISCOURSE?

POLITICAL ECONOMY AND THE GREAT IRISH FAMINE

TADHG FOLEY

This essay is part of the interdisciplinary series *Famine Folios*,
covering many aspects of the Great Hunger in Ireland from 1845–52.

CONTENTS

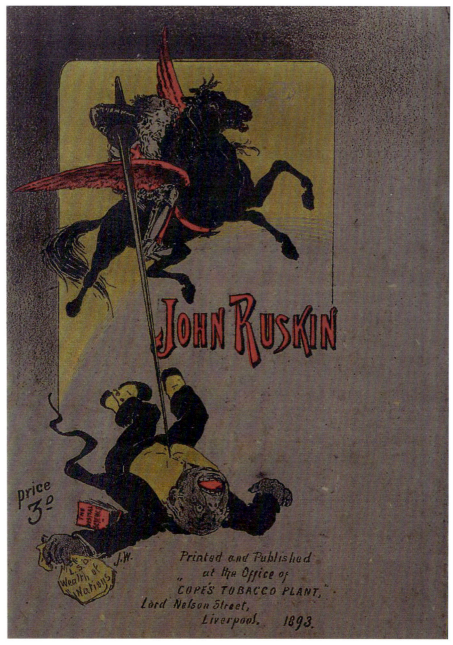

Figure 2 | John Wallace, cover of *John Ruskin, John Ruskin on Himself and Things in General*

INTRODUCTION

Though political economy (the old name for economics) was, for most of the nineteenth century, the sovereign public discourse in Britain, there was a widely held belief that it was "a science unknown in Ireland", or, if known, was not highly regarded.[1] There was intense and widespread controversy in Ireland concerning its role during the Famine, especially the policy of laissez-faire. For instance, it was alleged that ignorance or neglect of its principles contributed to causing the Famine, and there was extensive condemnation of the application (or too rigorous application) of these principles to a country for which they were deemed inappropriate, either because of the general circumstances of Ireland or because of its specific condition in the grip of famine. The debate surrounding the role of political economy in famine relief concerned matters of life and death, and raised fundamental moral and political questions, such as whether the right to subsistence was superior to that of property. But not only did political economy profoundly affect the Great Irish Famine, the Famine, in turn, influenced the subsequent fate of the discourse, forcing it to engage with the determining circumstances of time and place. A powerful moral critique of the discipline impugned its claim to be a science, while its historical contextualizing challenged the alleged universality of its laws, culminating in an evolutionary narrative that claimed that there were social formations to which political economy had no application whatever. But even in the land of its birth there was a vigorous moral critique of the discipline by authors such as Thomas Carlyle, Charles Dickens, and John Ruskin **[Figure 2]**.[2]

Charles Trevelyan, assistant secretary to the Treasury, was, in effect, in charge of famine–relief measures **[Figures 3 and 5]**. Both his diagnosis of, and cure for, Irish economic and social "ills" were in strict obedience to the tenets of political economy. As Eden Upton Eddis's 1850 portrait suggests, Trevelyan was a young man of fine features whose youthful elegance belies his unbending, doctrinaire personality. Firm–fisted and righteous, Trevelyan may look unsure of himself, but uncertainty never characterized his "duty" towards Ireland. The portrait was exhibited at the Royal Academy and considered a more suitable allusion to the Famine than Daniel Macdonald's shocking image of *An Irish Peasant Family Discovering the Blight of their Store*, shown in the British Institution just three years previously.

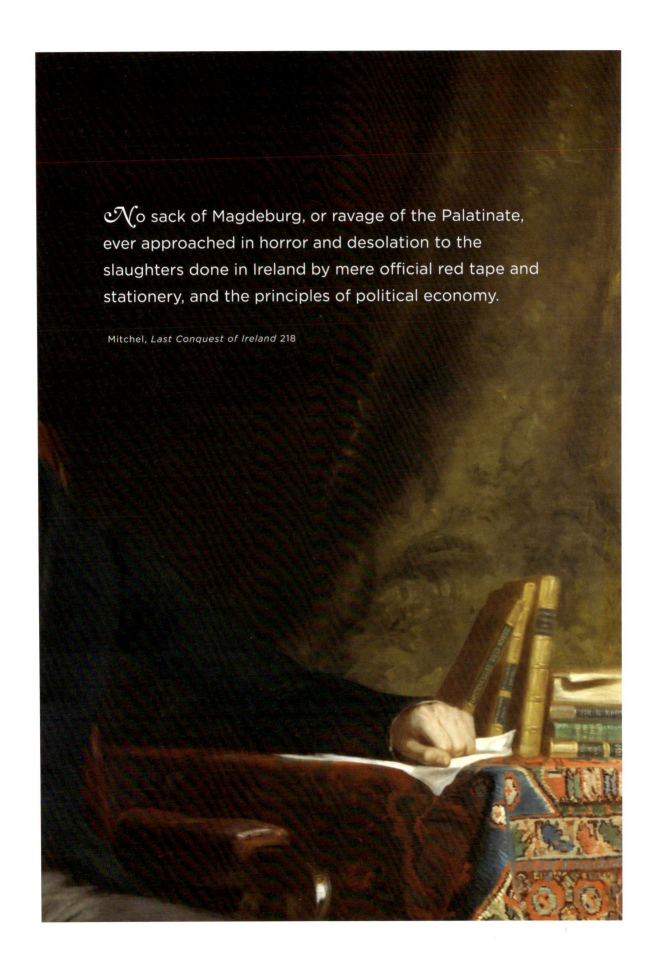

*N*o sack of Magdeburg, or ravage of the Palatinate,
ever approached in horror and desolation to the
slaughters done in Ireland by mere official red tape and
stationery, and the principles of political economy.

Mitchel, *Last Conquest of Ireland* 218

Political economy saw Ireland as economically backward, being overpopulated, seriously lacking in industry, and virtually totally dependent on a grossly inefficient agricultural sector. The modernization – in effect the anglicization – of Irish agriculture meant the substitution of capitalist farming for the cottier system, resulting in the consolidation of small farms into larger holdings, and the general replacement of tillage with pasture, resulting in human clearances to make way for cattle and sheep. The economic "backwardness" of Ireland was seen as both a cause and an effect of a flawed people, so that their mutual reformation presented challenges of an unusually formidable kind. Irish problems were held to arise not from social, political, or economic structures but from moral defects in the Irish character, such as indolence, improvidence, and a tendency towards disorder and lawlessness. The abject dependence of the Irish on others needed transformation into a sturdy self-reliance. They lacked perseverance, their labor was spasmodic and unfocused, and even their emigration was sporadic and random, a travesty of systematic colonization. The ubiquitous potato, root of all evil, was not only an inferior food – lacking the nutritional virtues of corn, not to mention roast beef – but also had deleterious effects on Irish character. It was described as the "lazy root", a characteristic it shared with the beds in which it was cultivated and with the people who planted and consumed it. It grew abundantly, even in inferior soil, and demanded very little labor, thereby contributing to the celebrated laziness of the Irish people while providing them with sufficient time and energy for a little sedition and nocturnal conspiracy. Political economy was given a central role in the transformation – cultural and agricultural – of Ireland, the "rationalization" of land, and the intimately connected radical amelioration of Irish character, and a powerful campaign to promote it was conducted in Ireland, beginning in the early 1830s.

Figure 3 | Eden Upton Eddis, *Sir Charles Edward Trevelyan, 1st Bt (1809–1886)* [Detail]

EASY LESSONS

ON

MONEY MATTERS;

FOR THE

USE OF YOUNG PEOPLE.

LESSON I.

———

MONEY.

LESSON II.

———

EXCHANGES.

LESSON III.

———

COMMERCE.

LESSON IV.

———

COIN.

LESSON V.

———

OF VALUE.

PART I.

Lesson VI.

———

WAGES.

Part I.

Lesson VI.

———

WAGES.

Part II.

Lesson VII.

———

RICH AND POOR.

Part I.

Lesson VIII.

———

CAPITAL.

Part I.

Lesson IX.

———

TAXES.

Part I.

Lesson X.

———

LETTING AND HIRING.

Part I.

Figure 4 | Richard Whately, images from title pages of *Easy Lessons on Money Matters; For the Use of Young People*

DISSEMINATION OF POLITICAL ECONOMY

Free trade, and free markets generally, were clearly in the interests of the first industrialized and the richest country in the world, already in possession of a vast empire. Crucially, political economy was also the discourse that theorized and justified colonization. It claimed scientific impartiality, its laws being objective, of universal validity, unchangeable, and beyond contestation. Edmund Burke, in words widely cited during the Famine, spoke of "the laws of commerce, which are the laws of nature, and consequently the laws of God" (32). The removal of the patently ideological adjective "political" helped to advance the discipline's claim to be a science. In the 1870s the term "economics" took over and its scientific status was seen to be copper-fastened with the mathematicizing of many of its procedures.

Beginning in the early 1830s, there was a systematic crusade against the ungodly economic ignorance and unbelief of the Irish, its leading evangelist Richard Whately, archbishop of Dublin. Like his friend Nassau Senior, he propagated neither the classical cost-of-production nor labor theories of value, but, in effect, a harsher, consumer-focused theory that eventually culminated in the notion of consumer sovereignty. In 1832 Whately founded and funded the Whately Chair of Political Economy in Trinity College, Dublin. Subsequently, the most important contribution to the teaching of political economy in Ireland was the foundation of the Queen's Colleges in 1845, as each of the colleges (at Belfast, Cork, and Galway) had a chair of jurisprudence and political economy. The Board of National Education was established in 1831, mainly to provide elementary education for the poor, and Whately became its effective chairman after 1832. He did not consider it beneath archiepiscopal dignity to write *Easy Lessons on Money Matters* [Figure 4] for schoolchildren, the nineteenth-century's best-selling text on political economy. The subject was preached to the poor of Ireland through the Barrington Lectures, established in 1834 but in abeyance until 1849 when their administration was taken over by the Dublin Statistical Society, established in 1847, at the height of the Famine. Whereas the discussion of economic theory was deemed appropriate to university chairs, the Statistical Society's mission was primarily the application of economic theories to practical problems. Public lectures were delivered before the society and published in its *Transactions of the Dublin Statistical Society* and, later, *Journal of the Dublin Statistical Society*. During the Famine, all of these institutions combined to defend the principles of political economy, then under unrelenting attack.

CONDITION OF IRELAND

The classical school of political economy was virtually unanimous in its views on Ireland until the later writings of John Elliot Cairnes and John Stuart Mill. The pivotal concept of the theory of distribution was the relation between population and capital that was crucial to the classical analyses of wages and profits. In Ireland, in the virtual absence of industry, land was the crucial economic resource. The increase in population had far outstripped the growth of capital; as a result, the average rate of wages fell to a minimum subsistence level, and, combined with the virtual absence of employment opportunities outside of agriculture, created intense competition for land, leading to subdivision (with consequent population growth) and rack-renting. A fundamental condition for any economic development was an alteration of the population/capital ratio through increasing capital or reducing population, or a combination of the two.

POPULATION: Commentators such as James Anthony Lawson argued that underproduction rather than overpopulation was Ireland's problem. Though he disapproved of state intervention, he had absolute confidence in an even higher outside agency, holding that the "march of population may be safely left to the guidance of ... Providence" (76). Classical economists were almost unanimously opposed to the introduction of a general system of poor relief because it would encourage population growth. Given their low estimate of Irish character, they had little confidence in Malthus's "preventative checks" of moral restraint through abstinence and delayed marriage, advocating instead agricultural improvement, in particular the substitution of corn and grass for potatoes. Overwhelmingly they advocated emigration, which was dramatically complemented by Malthus's "positive checks" of starvation and disease. The Irish peasant's minimal wants were seen to exacerbate population growth, since "the Irish peasant who was content with a bed of straw and a dinner of potatoes, and whose skill consisted in the use of a spade, could marry at eighteen" (Hearn, *Plutology* 393).

CAPITAL: The deficient supply of capital was seen as the inevitable consequence of the lack of security of property in Ireland, whose "pacification" was fortuitously enabled by famine through starvation and exile, though even the dead did not always rest in peace. Foresight and abstinence were as crucial to capital accumulation as to population control, but were sadly lacking in Irish character. Potato cultivation, needing virtually no capital, had to be superseded by corn, which required both capital and morally transformed cultivators, and, indeed, in some cases morally redeemed landlords. In societies blessed with civility, culture was conceived of as descending from the upper orders to the common people, but in Ireland its trajectory was often held to be in the opposite direction. Defying gravity, the baleful influence of the Irish lower classes (the all-too-perfect exemplars of national character) flowed upwards, seriously contaminating their betters, and morally encumbering them. In addition, conventionally encumbered landlords needed to be replaced by a capitalist landed class, one morally qualified and preferably originating in England or Scotland. That elite version of emigration and unpunished form of vagrancy known as absenteeism, where landlords "frequently estranged themselves even bodily" from Ireland ("An Ulsterman" 15), was widely condemned **[Figure 1]**. The Encumbered Estates Court was set up in 1849 to establish a new commercial and modernizing landlord class **[Figure 6]**.

PEEL'S PANACEA FOR IRELAND.

Russell. "OH! THIS DREADFUL IRISH TOOTHACHE!"
Peel. "WELL, HERE IS SOMETHING THAT WILL CURE YOU IN AN INSTANT."

Figure 6 | "Peel's Panacea for Ireland" (*Punch*, vol. xvi, 1849)

LAND: The supply of land could be increased by the reclamation of waste lands, also known as home colonization. Ireland, sometimes called the "Urinal of the Planets", was so identified with its bogs that it came to be "humorously" referred to as "Bog-land", its inhabitants "Bog-landers", with the more energetic of the race seen as "Bog-trotters" **[Figure 7]**. Bogs, standing for atavism and backwardness, needed to be drained to become *terra firma*, though *The Times* remarked that "human drainage" was "the only drainage an Irish landlord will ever think of doing at his own expense" (May 8, 1847, qtd. in Donnelly 125). Ebenezer Shackleton, distinguishing between productive and unproductive expenditure, remarked dryly that "draining bottles and draining land" impacted differentially on the wealth of nations (4). For Carlyle, bogs were "ugly as chaos" and resistant to human lordship: "Abominable bog, thou *shalt* cease to be abominable, and become subject to man!" (qtd. in McLean 47). Drainage subdued the bogs, an essential component of the colonial mission to discipline, civilize, and make rational not only Irish people but Irish landscape **[Figure 8]**. However, in Carlyle's opinion, only English and Scottish settlers were "viable agents of its subjugation" (McLean 47). For Froude, the Irish temperament was "Unstable as water", so doubtless it, too, required draining to achieve constancy and solidity (Brady 264).

The supply of land was seen as restricted by legislation respecting occupation and ownership, problems with title and registration, and the high cost of transfer, as well

Figure 7 | William Elmes, *Irish Bogtrotters*

as the entails and settlements that inhibited alienation. Most classical economists believed that a more efficient agriculture could be achieved only through the replacement of Ireland's cottier system with the capitalist leasehold tenancy on the English model. This would involve a large injection of capital and the removal of population to facilitate the consolidation of farms. Trevelyan declared that "The master evil of the agricultural system of Ireland, however, is the law of Entail, and the Incumbrances which seldom fail to accumulate upon entailed estates" (25–6). William Neilson Hancock condemned entails and other restraints on the power of alienation, whose chief object was "to maintain a wealthy and hereditary aristocracy" ("Economic causes" 9). Entails represented the past, the dominion of the dead; land should become bourgeois property, a commodity like any other.

THE NEW IRISH STILL.

SHOWING HOW ALL SORTS OF GOOD THINGS MAY BE OBTAINED (BY INDUSTRY) OUT OF PEAT.

Figure 8 | "The New Irish Still" (*Punch*, vol. xvii, 1849)

CONSOLIDATION: The Famine was a godsend for modernization, ridding the country of starving tenants, facilitating consolidation, and replacing encumbered landlords. Trevelyan condemned the "barbarous Irish tenure called *Rundale*" (25), a rundale or clachan being a "nucleated group of farmhouses, where land-holding was organised communally" (Whelan 453). Improving observers condemned clachans as (like the ubiquitous pig) dirty and disorderly, just as the potato was a "dirty weed" and a "porcine root"; this patchwork system of landholding resembled the rags worn by the people and the ruins that disfigured the landscape. Thomas Scott, an English land agent, denounced the "higgledy-piggledy mixture of fields" in Lord Audley's former estate in west Cork, and "consolidated" them into new farms (Hickey 199–200). The anglicization of Irish soil, not only economic but also aesthetic, involved a disciplining of landscape, making the crooked ways straight, with the disorder and irregularity of rundale villages giving way to straight lines, enclosure, and individual farms. For observers such as Carlyle, fenced fields represented civilization, whereas unenclosed, unfenced ones signified primitive, anarchic liberty. Ironically, this rooting out of what one might call "pig order" was in obedience to political economy, which was grounded in utilitarianism, famously derided by Carlyle as "pig philosophy". The clachan was *terra nullius*, no man's land, as it was not individually owned. As Kevin Whelan remarks, "Behind these conceptions lay the colonial fantasy of the *tabula rasa* – a clean Irish slate on which the new English values could be legibly inscribed" (464). Indeed, Rev. Edward Nangle's "Colony" converted a part of Achill Island to Rupert Brooke's "some corner of a foreign field / That is for ever England" **[Figure 9]**. The Famine, in its destruction of the clachan system, gratifyingly contributed to order, progress, and linearity.

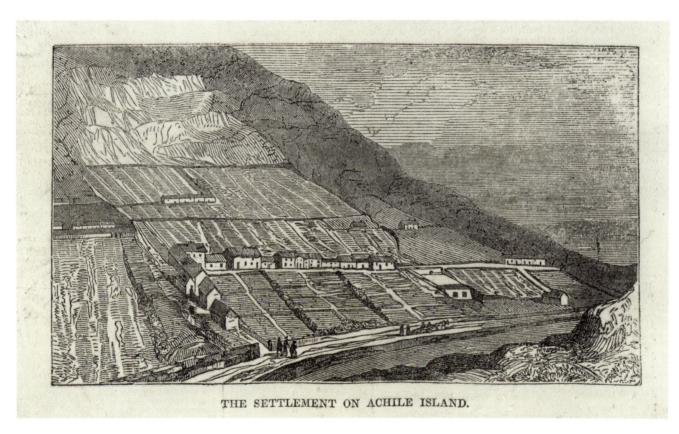

THE SETTLEMENT ON ACHILE ISLAND.

Figure 9 | "The Settlement on Achile [*sic*] Island" (*Pictorial Times*, November 7, 1846)

IRISH CHARACTER

For many, the ultimate cause of the Famine was not simply the palpable economic state of Ireland but the more mediated and intangible agency of Irish character, seen as metaphysically given rather than as historically produced, and the cause rather than the effect of poverty. A later writer put the matter bluntly, invoking the authority of science: "Some politicians harp unceasingly upon unjust laws, unhappy circumstances, etc. etc., when the real thing that wants remedying is the moral character of a degraded race of men" (Anon. 14).

Like their potatoes, the Irish were remarkably fecund, rooted in time and place, and mired in the past. They were what they ate. As Lord Clarendon, the viceroy, wrote to Russell, the "wretched people" seemed "to be human potatoes, a sort of emanation from 'the root' – they have lived by it and will die with it" (qtd. in Gray, *Famine, Land and Politics* 323) **[Figures 10 and 11]**. They were also like their pigs, the least transcendent of all animals, famously flightless, the earth their element. Potatoes were sometimes called "murphies", and the *Oxford English Dictionary* informs us that a "Murphy's countenance" was a "pig's face". The religion of the Irish, often characterized as superstitious and idolatrous, was earthbound, too, for, according to the *Achill Missionary Herald* (August, 1846), Catholics "worship the work of their own hands, that which their own fingers have made" (qtd. in O'Rourke 514). The unreformed religion subscribed to by the majority of the people of Ireland was seen as a key determinant of Irish character and by certain authorities as a cause of the Great Famine. O'Rourke gives some evidence for this view (514–16), including a letter written by Dickens in the autumn of 1846 and published in John Forster's *The Life of Charles Dickens*. He had been visiting the Simplon valley, and described where a Protestant canton ended and a Catholic one began. Here, he wrote,

you might separate two perfectly distinct and different conditions of humanity, by drawing a line with your stick in the dust on the ground. On the Protestant side, neatness; cheerfulness; industry; education; continual aspiration, at least, after better things. On the Catholic side, dirt; disease; ignorance; squalor; and misery. I have so constantly observed the like of this, since I first came abroad, that I have a sad misgiving, that the religion of Ireland lies as deep at the root of all her sorrows even as English misgovernment and Tory villainy (qtd. in O'Rourke 516).

THE REAL POTATO BLIGHT OF IRELAND.

(FROM A SKETCH TAKEN IN CONCILIATION HALL.)

Figure 10 | "The Real Potato Blight of Ireland (From a Sketch Taken in Conciliation Hall)" (*Punch*, vol. ix, 1845)

A SKETCH OF THE GREAT AGI-TATER

Figure 11 | Henry Heath (Paul Pry). *A Sketch of the Great Agi-tater*

WANTING WANTS: An important failure of character was that the Irish "wanted wants", a sure sign of savagery or barbarism, an embarrassment to political economy. Hearn's *Plutology* pioneered the concept of the centrality of wants as the engine of economic activity. In his view, "those nations, and those classes of a nation who stand highest in the scale of civilization, are those whose wants, as experience shows us, are the most numerous; and whose efforts to satisfy those wants are the most unceasing" (20).

REMITTANCES: Another example of the failure of the Irish to meet with the requirements of political economy was their self-abnegation, especially as manifested in their hospitality and in the remittances emigrants sent home to their families. This "family and clan feeling" was often seen as a vestige of archaic society, and, for some, a strong indication that the spirit of the Brehon laws endured in the hearts of the people. Hearn stated in *The Aryan Household*, "I need not cite authorities in support of so well known a fact as the absolute self-abnegation of the Keltic clansman" (201). But it was precisely this self-abnegation that was seen to be disastrous for economic progress and modernity. The Irish had an insufficiently developed sense of the individual and individual self-interest – an economically catastrophic failure of character.

DIET: Not only had the potato to suffer the indignity of being categorized by political economists as an "inferior good" – one the consumption of which falls as incomes rise – but it was also condemned for its frequent failures and as a "dirty weed", deficient in dietary terms, marooned (like the Irish themselves) in time and space, and resistant to being stored or transported. In Ireland, victory in the evolutionary struggle for existence in the vegetable kingdom went to the potato, a potent example of the survival of the unfittest in that benighted country. No less an authority on the tuber than Trevelyan could ask, "But what hope is there for a nation which lives on potatoes?" (2). Hancock took issue with Trevelyan, quoting Mountifort Longfield's acerbic remark that "Such language ... would be more applicable, *if they eat men instead of feeding them*" (qtd. in "Notice" 8). Commissary general, Sir Randolph Routh, like Trevelyan, wanted the potato to be reduced to mere vegetative status, and "in time resume its proper station as a vegetable, and cease to be a staple article of food" (qtd. in Gray, *Famine, Land and Politics* 119).

But the alimentary criticisms of the potato were minor in comparison with the furious assault on the alleged social, economic, and cultural consequences of potato cultivation. The anonymous author of *What Science Is Saying about Ireland*, guided by racial science, advocated "carefully avoiding legislation that may in any way favour dependence upon a root that can only produce a race of men in type on a par with or perhaps even lower than the negro" (51). In Trevelyan's words, "The relations of employer and employed, which knit together the framework of society, and establish a mutual dependence and good-will, have no existence in the potato system. The Irish small holder lives in a state of isolation" (5). These views were shared by a more sympathetic observer, Isaac Butt, for whom "The worst of this mode of subsistence was, that it shut out the man who so existed from any contact with the mercantile and social world" (32).

Part of the argument against the potato was that it could be cultivated in most soils, required little labor, capital, or skill, and needed only boiling to become food. But Satan made work for idle hands, and, as John Hall put it, "Time was when, the potatoes having been planted, the cultivator had little to do but watch their growth by day, and do a little secret society work at night" (59). This nocturnal social interaction might be thought to compensate for barbaric daytime isolation, but it failed to gain official approval. Routh stated that "The little industry called for to rear the potato, and its prolific growth, leave the people to indolence and all kinds of vice, which habitual labour and a higher order of food would prevent" (qtd. in Kinealy, *Calamity* 52). These problems could be solved by a move from potatoes to corn, but, in Trevelyan's words, "The change from an idle, barbarous isolated potato cultivation, to corn cultivation, which frees industry, and binds together employer and employee in mutually beneficial relations ... requires capital and a new class of men" (qtd. in Kinealy, *Great Irish Famine* 19). Or, in a further ascent of the alimentary hierarchy, what one might call "cornivores" could aspire to becoming carnivores, also with additional gratifying cultural consequences. According to *The Times* (September 22, 1846):

For our part, we regard the potato blight as a blessing. When the Celts once cease to be potatophagi, they must become carnivorous. With the taste of meats will grow the appetite for them; with the appetite, the readiness to earn them. With this will come steadiness, regularity, and perseverance (qtd. in Gray, *Famine, Land and Politics* 227).

GOG AND MAGOG GIVING PADDY A LIFT OUT OF THE MIRE.

"A Special Court of Common Council was held on Thursday to consider the propriety of purchasing estates in Ireland, with a view to cultivate and improve the same. * *.* That London can and will do this work, her own history affords the most abundant guarantees."

Vide "Times," July 7.

Figure 12 | "Gog and Magog Giving Paddy a Lift Out of the Mire" (*Punch*, vol. xvii, 1849)

REFORMATION OF IRISH CHARACTER

For the Irish, progress of any kind could only be achieved by external intervention. Indeed, for Trevelyan, "the only hope for those who lived upon potatoes was in some great intervention of Providence" (8). For this subterranean society, cultural redemption, too, came from "some other quarter" (ultramarine rather than ultramontane), from Providence's visible representative on earth, Ireland's civilized neighbor. In Whately's view:

the savage himself, though he may be, as it were, a soil capable of receiving the seeds of civilization, can never, in the first instance, produce it, as of spontaneous growth; and unless those seeds be introduced from some other quarter, must remain forever in the sterility of barbarism (*Introductory Lectures* 112).

In the opinion of George Cornwall Lewis, in Ireland "Improvement and civilization must there descend from above; they will not rise spontaneously from the inward workings of the community" (v-vi). But a "lift" could also come from below **[Figure 12]**. The gifts from on high, if they were to quell primitive anarchy, could only be conferred by discipline of both body and mind, and political economy was a particularly severe taskmaster.

DISCIPLINE: There was a formidable array of both repressive and ideological state apparatuses to discipline the Irish, as David Nally enumerates: "Centralised political administration, a unified police force, paid magistrates, public dispensaries, a unified and regulated network of lunatic asylums, and state-backed elementary schooling – this was a massive undertaking requiring new regimes of calculation and surveillance" (100). There was a shift towards what Senior called "central superintendence" (99), Europe's colonies acting as "laboratories of modernity" (98). Indeed, a strong interventionist state was needed to establish and maintain a regime of laissez-faire. In the new social order, competition provided moral education, and discipline was enforced by the mechanism of the market. For instance, George Nicholls, an English Poor Law Commissioner, felt that the introduction of strict, well-managed, and disciplinarian workhouses would improve "the character, habits and social condition of the people" (qtd. in Kinealy, *Calamity* 22). To Nally's "new regimes of calculation and surveillance", such as the Ordnance Survey, could be added the state-friendly Dublin Statistical Society. Mitchel writes that a "great leading idea" of Peel's policy was "to make the famine a strictly Government concern. It was to be administered strictly through officers of the Government, from high commissioners down to policemen". Such measures

led many persons to the conclusion that the enemy had resolved to avail themselves of the famine in order to increase Governmental supervision and espionage, so that every man, woman, and child in Ireland, with all their goings out and comings in, might be thoroughly known and registered; that when the mass of the people began to starve, their sole resource might be the police barracks; that Government might be all in all – omnipotent to give food or withhold it, to relieve or to starve, according to their own ideas of policy, and of good behaviour in the people (*History of Ireland* 210).

There was resistance to this discipline, and Shafto Adair speaks of the growing Famine as driving "the wretched beings, who overcame, alas! too late, their abhorrence of the confinement and regularity of the Union houses, to the detested refuge" (24–5). But such discipline would usher in a new dispensation where "Prudence and thrift are practised on a large scale; regularity and order take the place of spontaneous intermittent exertion, and the new custom is ranked among the decencies of civilized life" (49).

PEASANT PROPRIETORSHIP: For John Locke, the theorist of private property, freedom meant the property of oneself, and he defended liberty in order to guarantee property. Trevelyan, unexceptionally, believed that the Irish, emotionally incontinent, lacked the self-possession necessary to qualify for a regime of peasant proprietorship:

A peasant proprietary may succeed to a certain extent, where there is a foundation of steadiness of character, and a habit of prudence, and a spring of pride, and a value for independence and comfort; but we fear that all these words merely show the vain nature of schemes of peasant proprietorship for Ireland (175).

Longfield also held this position, but Cairnes, accepting that the Irish character was "careless" and "improvident", argued that it was historically produced and that "peasant proprietorship appears to me to be exactly the specific for the prevailing Irish disease" (Mill 1081).

DEFENSE OF POLITICAL ECONOMY

According to Whately's first biographer, at "a moment when all Ireland was drilling, and Dublin seemed like a slumbering volcano, the Archbishop propounded a panacea against the threatened siege" – political economy, and he strongly urged Young Ireland to study it (Fitzpatrick 63, 67–8). This advice was given at the Dublin Statistical Society on June 19, 1848. At the same meeting Whately spoke of political economy as the "*only* means which existed of rescuing the country from convulsion". "It was a mistake to suppose", he argued,

that religion or morals alone would be sufficient to save a people from revolution. No; they would not be sufficient, if a proper idea of Political Economy was not cultivated by that people. A man, even of the purest mind and most exalted feelings, without a knowledge of Political Economy, could not be secured from being made instrumental in forwarding most destructive and disastrous revolutions ("Report" 5).

The establishment vigorously defended political economy, and the market as a sacrosanct, self-regulating mechanism. It was argued that *too much* state intervention, not *too little*, was the cause of Ireland's misery, and that only free trade in food could counteract the Famine.

According to Peter Gray, Trevelyan was "conscious of the need to reassure his wavering subordinates, and bombarded them with didactic literature". A special edition of Adam Smith's "Digression Concerning the Corn Trade and Corn Laws" was issued "to every Commissariat officer and clerk". Trevelyan was particularly impressed by Smith's arguments that it was price controls that produced, "instead of the hardships of a dearth, the dreadful horrors of a famine". Trevelyan sent extracts from Burke's *Thoughts and Details on Scarcity* (Gray, *Famine, Land and Politics* 254), and he also dispatched his own articles and book to relief officials in Ireland (Kinealy, *Calamity* 418).

Hancock published a book in 1847 with the challenging title *Three Lectures on the Questions: Should the Principles of Political Economy Be Disregarded at the Present*

Crisis? The answer was a resounding "no". According to Hancock, the hard-headed principles of political economy pointed out that "providing food *for sale* in *all* districts, and under *all* circumstances, should be left to the foresight and enterprise of private merchants" (19). The "deaths in the west of Ireland, instead of proving the danger of too strict an adherence to sound principles, prove the danger of any departure, however slight, from such principles" (22).

RELIGION: Though the defenders of political economy descanted endlessly on its strict scientific credentials and its independence of religious and moral discourses, they were anxious to assert its compatibility with "true" religion and morality. In the preface to his *Introductory Lectures*, Whately says, "It has been my first object, to combat the prevailing prejudices against the study; and especially those which represent it as unfavourable to Religion". By the "wise arrangements of Providence, not only self-interest, but in some instances even the most sordid selfishness, are made, in an advanced stage of society, to conduce to public prosperity" (viii, 145), an elegant variation of the theological doctrine of *felix culpa*, the fortunate fall. For Hancock it was inappropriate, if not immoral, to describe economists as "*hard-hearted and cruel*". For him there was a preordained harmony between the laws of political economy and the laws of God, for the call for government interference in the price of provisions "generally arises from the common prejudice, which attributes the rise in price to the conduct of the dealers in provisions, instead of to the wisdom of the Almighty" (*Three Lectures* 12, 51).

MORALITY: As well as being compatible with religion, political economy also laid claim to being a moral discourse. Individual hedonism was miraculously transubstantiated into social utility, and greed – universally excoriated by moralists – was indeed good. The market was held to deliver not merely efficiency but morality. As Alexander Somerville put it, "Political economy is in itself the very essence of humanity, benevolence, and justice" (134). According to Hearn, "The principle of competition then may fairly claim to be described as beneficent, just, and equalizing" (*Plutology* 338–9), composing the cacophony of conflicting private interests into the harmony of the common good. Hobbes's war of "every man against every man" in the state of nature was continued in civil society, powerfully enhanced by Malthus's theory of population, and subsequently by the Darwinian doctrine of the struggle for existence. Competition was the basis of civil society, and it alone guaranteed human progress and civilization. This mutual antagonism was the engine of history, awakening all the powers of humanity unaroused by Arcadian harmony. Just as there was a preordained concord between the sacred and profane, between the laws of God and the "dismal science", between virtue and interests, there was also a "harmony of interests". According to Hancock:

Such are the manifest conclusions of economic science, the dissemination of which is calculated to produce happiness, contentment, and peace – teaching, as they do, individuals, classes, and nations that the true interest of each is the true interest of all; that one class can never be sacrificed to another with impunity ("Economic views" 13).

Hancock condemned Butt for subversively speaking of the "monopolizing power of wealth", and for "freely and unreservedly" advocating "the right of the artisan to protection against the grinding influence of riches" ("Economic views" 12).

CORN DEALERS: Corn dealers or factors were often accused of heartlessly barring their doors until the price of corn increased. Hancock defended them on the basis of the "well-established economic principle, that the interest of consumers and that of producers are really the same" ("Economic views" 9). But class conflict was structurally impossible in this version of political economy. Unfortunately, the unreflecting (then very numerous in Ireland) did not perceive "the wisdom of the Almighty, in making the security of the most vital interests of the community depend not on any general benevolence or public spirit, but on the strongest and most enduring of human motives – self interest" (*Three Lectures* 61).

Judging by the political-economy papers in the examinations for male National teachers in 1848 and during the immediate post-Famine years, the activities of the corn dealers were felt to be in dire need of justification. In 1848, for example, the following question was asked: "What is the illustration made use of to show the beneficial action of the corn dealer upon the market of provisions, in times of scarcity?" (Commissioners of National Education in Ireland 305). Whately and many others strenuously defended the widely excoriated "meal-mongers".

PROPERTY: Central to the mission of political economy was the defense of private property. For Longfield it was a "false and dangerous" doctrine to maintain that "extreme want" justified a "disregard of the rights of property" (29). The examination in political economy for male National teachers in 1848 and subsequent years reflected these ideological anxieties. The redistribution of wealth was described as "robbery" and "spoliation", and the unambiguous agenda of the questions was to undermine cost of production and especially labor theories of value, and to deny the state any redistributive function. It defended the sacredness of property and the blessings of inequality, chief among which was that inequality enabled charity, a view we are told several times was supported by the Apostles. If the poor did not exist, the propensity of the rich towards being charitable would sadly have remained unexercised. Charity benefitted the poor materially and the rich spiritually as an "investment" in the afterlife, and, as a bonus, helped to counteract communism, a great threat to the starving Irish in the 1840s (Commissioners of National Education in Ireland 290, 299, 303, 305). Whately asked if the poor would be better off were the property of the rich divided among them. No, he concluded, "All would soon be as miserably poor as the most destitute beggars are now. Indeed, far worse, *there would be nobody to beg of*" (*Easy Lessons* 48). Not only did the rich enjoy their wealth in this life but the sacrifice they made in giving to the poor was an investment in eternal life. For the archbishop, the wealthy, regardless of their actions or intentions, were social benefactors; if they chose to practice charity, they were twice-blessed.

CRITIQUE OF POLITICAL ECONOMY

The critique of political economy reached its greatest intensity at the time of the Famine. Systematic Irish nationalist opposition could be said to date from the foundation of *The Nation* newspaper in 1842. No wonder Whately "strongly advised" the Young Irelanders to study political economy. The revolutionary nationalist papers, in addition to giving instructions in small-arms drill and street fighting, mercilessly attacked political economy and especially its great crusader, Whately, whose former friend at Oxford, John Henry Newman, wrote that political economy was a "science at the same time dangerous and leading to occasions of sin" (86). Catholic teaching was virtually unanimous in its critique of the science. John Hughes, bishop of New York, for instance, denied that the Famine was a "mysterious visitation of God's providence" and blamed political economy, which authorized the provision merchant "even amidst the desolation, to keep his doors locked, and his sacks of corn tied up within, waiting for a better price"(21), for the "sacredness of the rights of property must be maintained at all sacrifices, unless we would have society to dissolve itself into its original elements" (22). But for Hughes

the rights of life are dearer and higher than those of property; and in a general famine like the present, there is no law of Heaven, nor of nature, that forbids a starving man to seize on bread wherever he can find it, even though it should be the loaves of proposition on the altar of God's temple (22).

And, according to a "Memorial of the Catholic Bishops and Archbishops of Ireland" in October 1847, "the sacred and indefeasible rights of life are forgotten amidst the incessant reclamation of the subordinate rights of property" (qtd. in Gray, *Famine, Land and Politics* 142).

The reform of land tenure and a condemnation of laissez-faire and free trade were the central concerns of Irish-nationalist economic writings. But frequently this opposition went far beyond individual economic issues to a root-and-branch critique of political economy and of its philosophical underpinning, utilitarianism. Nationalist reaction ranged from an almost complete rejection of political economy to a demand for the relaxation of its laws in the exceptional circumstances of Ireland (especially in the throes of famine) and, as in the case of Mitchel, a demand for an "Irish" political economy.

Routh told a deputation from Achill that the government was determined "not to interfere with the merchants, but to act more in accordance with the enlightened principles of political economy". Fr Monahan said he could not understand why the government "was to be fettered by notions of political economy at such a crisis as this", but Routh replied that "nothing was more essential to the welfare of a country than strict adherence to free trade" (qtd. in O'Rourke 222–3). The people of Achill asked for bread and were given, if not stones, their discursive equivalent, a lecture on political economy. In 1847 the Irish Confederation published a small book, edited by John Mitchel, with extracts from Swift and Berkeley, entitled *Irish Political Economy*. Mitchel, who wrote elsewhere of "a nation perishing of political economy" (*History of Ireland* 218), contrasted "Irish" political economy with what he called "English" or "famine" political economy. Hancock replied that the "idea of having a science of exchanges peculiar to Ireland, under the name Irish Political Economy, is about as reasonable as proposing to have Irish mechanics, Irish mathematics, or Irish astronomy" ("Economic views" 3).

Butt was the only significant political economist to advocate protectionism and state intervention. The lectures on which he based his *Protection to Home Industry: Some Cases of its Advantages Considered* were delivered in 1840 but not published until 1846, and the book was approvingly reviewed in *The Nation* under the heading "Political economy for Ireland". His *A Voice for Ireland: The Famine in the Land* appeared shortly afterwards, declaring in dramatic capital letters that "either the general resources of the country must be called into immediate and vigorous activity, or Irish poverty supported for a time (and it can be but for a time) by the confiscation of Irish property" (iv). Calling for the revival and establishment of Irish manufactures, Butt stated that "we cannot help regarding as a great and a fatal mistake the determination to leave the supply of food entirely to the chances of private enterprise" (7).

The most concerted attacks on political economy, often from a class perspective, occurred in the pages of the revolutionary newspapers of 1848, the *United Irishman*, the *Irish Tribune*, and the *Irish Felon*. The *United Irishman* declared that by the operation of "what are called the 'Principles of Political Economy', above one million Irish population (rendered 'surplus' by the potato rot) were got rid of quietly, legally, and constitutionally, last year" (February 26, 1848). Many attacks were made on Whately, especially in a series of articles in the *United Irishman* entitled "Educational police" that focused centrally on his role in propagating political economy. The final article defended the working classes against political economy, describing the "rights of property" as a "sanctimonious" and "pharisaical" justification of plunder, and the doctrines of "fair competition" and "free trade" as "fraudulent" devices on the part of "capital to enable itself to perpetually rule and beat labour" (April 22, 1848). Overwhelmingly, the onslaught on political economy was moral; it had, in the words of Thomas Hood's "The Song of the Shirt" (slightly misquoted), "caused bread to be so dear, and flesh and blood so cheap" (April 29, 1848).

One could give countless examples of hostility towards political economy in the regional nationalist press. The *Galway Vindicator*, for example, berated Whately for propounding "crude theories in political economy – like those which starved the people in '47" (April 2, 1851). The same year it wrote scornfully of the "science of Adam Smith", which was used to "banish from Ireland the bone and sinew of the land" (March 8, 1851).

There were other voices, neither Irish nor nationalist, raised against the government's fetishization of political economy in dealing with the Famine. One such voice was that of the MP George Poulett Scrope, about whom Senior wrote that "Doctrines more subversive of property", and "therefore more subversive of government, of civilization, and of human morality and happiness, were never proclaimed by Fourier or by Owen, by Robespierre or by Babeuf" (qtd. in Nally 220). Lord George Bentinck argued for a relaxation of the "principles of political economy", stating that "non-interference with the import and retail trade may be good in ordinary times, but in times such as the present, when a calamity unexampled in the history of the world has suddenly fallen upon Ireland", the "severe rules of political economy" should be broken (qtd. in O'Rourke 301–2).

AFTER THE FAMINE

The Irish were unmoved by the "Easy Lessons" of Whately and the innumerable homilies on political economy preached for their edification, whereas the stern voice of nature attempted to impose, not always successfully, its allegedly irresistible "hard lessons" on them. According to a review of *The History of Famines in Ireland*, nature spoke "to man only through his sensations, his sufferings, and his joys; and at every period, by want, famine, pestilence, she has warned the Irish ... that they had done and were doing wrong". However, these warnings, though "terribly emphatic, have been misinterpreted or unheeded" by the Irish (*The Economist*, September 20, 1856). Senior wrote that the laboring population of every country was "condemned by nature to a life which is one struggle against want" (189). He added that "Hunger and cold are the punishments by which she [nature] represses improvidence and sloth. If we remove those punishments, we must substitute other means of repression" (190). Thus did Providence, through the vicarship of nature, attempt to repress Irish improvidence.

In a poem in the *Illustrated London News* (January 30, 1847), we find further sermons in stones:

> *But Nature vindicates her God;*
> *Teaches a lesson from the soil:*
> *A voice springs from the blighted sod*
> *In mercy for the sons of toil*
> (qtd. in Gray, "British public opinion" 93).

Adair also invokes the stern tutorship of nature, "the sad lesson which may be daily read in Ireland" and "the terrible schooling which is now being impressed in ineffaceable characters on the minds of all men" (3–4). Lord George Hill wrote:

The Irish people have profited much by the Famine, the lesson was severe; but so rooted were they in old prejudices and old ways, that no teacher could have induced them to make the changes which this Visitation of Divine Providence has brought about, both in their habits of life and in their mode of agriculture (qtd. in Kinealy, *Calamity* 353).

THEODICY: Providential readings, as with Hill, saw the Famine as a *felix culpa*, a theodicy that, in Milton's words, sought to "justify the ways of God to men". The very strategic doctrine of redemption through suffering, in the largely Catholic doctrine of Purgatory, was appealed to by, for instance, the Chancellor of the Exchequer, Charles Wood, who wrote to Clarendon that, "except through a purgatory of misery and starvation, I cannot see how Ireland is to emerge into anything approaching either quiet or prosperity" (qtd. in Kinealy, *Death-dealing* 122). Routh thought it "very probable that we may derive much advantage from this present calamity" (qtd. in Kinealy, *Calamity* 52), and, as we have seen, because of its contribution to the improvement of Irish character, *The Times* declared that "For our part, we regard the potato blight as a blessing" (September 22, 1846). Elizabeth Smith, the wife of a Wicklow landowner, exclaimed at the prospect of consolidation, "What a revolution for good will this failure of cheap food cause" (qtd. in Nally 279). Some of the more bourgeois Catholic nationalists, such as Justin McCarthy and A. M. Sullivan, were not unappreciative of the positive outcomes of the Famine. Indeed, Sullivan noted that

HERE AND THERE;
Or, Emigration a Remedy.

Figure 13 | "Here and There; or, Emigration a Remedy" (*Punch*, vol. xv, 1848)

after the Famine "Providence, forethought, economy are studied and valued as they never were before" (qtd. in Morash 148).

According to Robert Torrens, the wisdom of the Almighty was also manifest in the timing of the Famine, so providing opportunities for emigration **[Figure 13]** and colonization:

By a remarkable coincidence – might it not be said by a compensating arrangement, a guiding manifestation of Providence – the staple food of Ireland has failed at a period, when the Crown possesses, in its foreign dependencies, regions of unoccupied and fertile country, capable of subsisting, in unfailing abundance, the perishing millions of the United Kingdom (6).

Lord Lansdowne's agent, William Steuart Trench, claimed that "Nothing but the successive failures of the potato … could have produced the emigration which will, I trust, give us room to become civilised" (qtd. in Donnelly 23). For Anthony Trollope, too, the "beneficent agency" of Famine provided much-needed *Lebensraum*:

Such having been the state of the country, such its wretchedness, a merciful God sent the remedy which might avail to arrest it; and we – we deprecated his wrath … If this beneficent agency did not from time to time disencumber our crowded places, we should ever be living in narrow alleys with stinking gutters, and supply of water at the minimum (67).

Like Alexander Pope, Trevelyan could pronounce "All partial evil, universal good":

Unless we are much deceived, posterity will trace up to that famine the commencement of a salutary revolution in the habits of a nation long singularly unfortunate, and will acknowledge that on this, as on many other occasions, Supreme Wisdom has educed permanent good out of transient evil (1).

SOCIAL EVOLUTION

After the Famine, the great moral critique of individualism in Ireland was conducted in the name of the family, with Hancock, in particular, celebrating the "wonderful and strong family and clan feeling" of the Irish ("Remittances" 287). Indeed, in 1859 he read a paper to the Dublin Statistical Society with the provocative title "The family and not the individual the true unit to be considered in social questions". Now he argued that "the care of wealth has now, as ever, a tendency to hardness of heart, which moral discipline is necessary to control", adding that "social science does not sanction any law of competition as a substitute for the important moral duties that devolve on every owner of wealth and every employer of labour" ("Bothy system" 381). One witness before a royal commission lamented the "foolish attachment to home" among the Irish (qtd. in Nally 210). According to another source, "The aboriginal Irish Celt is violently attached to his family and to the country and locality of his birth, and is therefore averse to emigration". Here Humboldt is quoted as saying that savages "know and care for only their own family; they know the ties of relationship, but not those of humanity" (Anon. 29–30). There was a recurring trope in the Victorian period that social bonding for the Irish (or, more generally, the Celts) was personal rather than civil, a matter of personal affiliation rather than the rule of law, a trope facilitated by the widespread gendering of Ireland as female. In general, the Celtic Irish, supposedly inherently aristocratic and devoted to persons rather than to institutions or abstract ideas, were mired in the local, the specific, and the present, and unable to ascend to the general and the universal, nor to extend their vision to the future, thus failing to master abstraction and being unable to make the transition from the domestic to the political, from nation to empire.

This "family affection" was seen as militating against capital accumulation, central to modernity and to a progressive society. Many authors, embracing new evolutionary ideas, saw Ireland as virtually an archaic society closer to its Aryan origins than to English commercial society. Basing his views on the researches of Sir Henry Maine, A. G. Richey saw early Irish society as a "community without a government or executive; without laws, in the modern sense of the term; in which the individual had no rights save as a member of a family", where private property scarcely existed and where social bonding was achieved not through law and contract but through custom. Richey held that trade in a family-centered society was "uninfluenced by the laws of political economy" (35). Hearn eventually challenged the universal character of economic laws, saying that "the conditions of political society alone furnish the postulates of political economy" (*Aryan Household* 10).

It was received wisdom in the second half of the nineteenth century that all Aryan societies went through the same evolutionary process but at widely differing speeds. The evolutionary narrative was of a unilineal, undialectical kind, a form of conquest or consumption, with each stage, in the usual biological model, devouring its predecessor, though that which was devoured might well retain a certain subversive intestine agency. The "undead" residues of earlier stages of evolution, the remains of clannish custom and tradition, were execrated as the detritus of history, but could also be seen as equivalent to the remnant of Israel, in whom future hope was vested (see Isaiah 10: 20–2). Philosophical tourists in Ireland had long expatiated critically on pigs, potatoes, and bogs, the refuse respectively of the animal, vegetable, and mineral kingdoms, as well as on ruins and rags, the debris of the built environment and human dress respectively. Picturesque tourists were more forgiving. For David Lloyd, what were seen as premodern residues were "rather the products of a continual and creative transformation, coeval but out of kilter with the imposed disciplines of modernization. They mark a counter-modern effect of modernity that haunts the modernizing subject" (155). As Luke Gibbons puts it, progress is pictured as spreading from the metropolitan center "to more backward, outlying regions, producing, at best, local inflections of the modern or, at worst, mere colonial mimicry of the master's voice". He suggests the possibility of "peripheral", "*alternative* or *discrepant* modernities, no less intent on determining their own futures as their dominant Western counterparts but not necessarily following in their footsteps" ("Peripheral" 272–3).

The notion of "governing Ireland according to Irish ideas" was advocated by Cairnes and Mill in the 1860s, and later gained fairly general acceptance, including by Gladstone himself. This alternative imperial strategy of "kindness" for modernizing Ireland contrasted with more robust alternatives advocated by others. Ireland was routinely figured as female, and so in need of protection, and childlike, and so needful of tuition. Mill's "government of leading strings" is related to his doctrine of the "infant industry" that advocated protectionism in certain circumstances. This meant that industry, having established itself under a regime of protection, could grow into independent adulthood. In dealings with Ireland in the late 1860s, there was a change in policy, instituted by Gladstone, from a Spartan to an Athenian strategy, from, as some would put it, masculine force to feminine kindness, an approach exemplified by the leading monger of kindness, Matthew Arnold. The Famine contributed, in no small measure, to changing Cairnes's thinking on the question of land from "English" to "Irish" ideas. In an extraordinary series of articles in *The Economist* in 1865, "Ireland in transition", he wrote that "English theory" was at variance with "Irish ideas" and did not explain Irish fact. He vigorously opposed the commodification of land, the sanctity of contract, and the absolute nature of private property in land – what he described as the "English doctrine" of "open competition and contract" (October 14, 1865). Many others defended "Irish ideas", such as "An Irish Liberal", who, looking back on the Famine in 1888, wrote that "Government interference, it was argued, would prejudice private enterprise. The laws of political economy, and the doctrine of *laissez-faire* were equal to all emergencies", adding dryly, "We know what happened" (46).

But Hearn considered protection to be a "killing kindness" (*Cassell Prize Essay* 83), while *The Times* also clearly disapproved of Mill's strategy of "leading strings":

The theory of relief was not to lead the Irish people on step by step until they could walk alone. A nation is not trained to manly virtue as an infant is taught to walk. A certain amount of misery and hardship [is necessary] … if they would be invulnerable to hostile attack. Had we persisted in the futile attempt to indoctrinate Ireland gradually into self-reliance, the morrow on which she was to have been liberated from tutelage would have never come (qtd. in Gray, "British public opinion" 68).

Condemning "Quaker quietism" (Anon. 10) and advocating "despotism (of course as benevolent as possible)" as the "only effectual government" (12), another author claimed that "The only chance for a savage to behave well and improve is by his being ruled well and strongly. As society and human character develop, men can be ruled by other masters, such as law, public opinion, conscience, noble passions and desires, etc." (9). However, there was, according to the same authority, "a strange idea afloat that every race of barbarians should be governed according to the ideas of that race" (57). These "Irish ideas" threatened to "unsettle the principles of Political Economy, to shake the stability of contracts as a law of civilised society, and to invade the rights of property" ("Political Economy" 2). The 1870 Irish Land Act had "violated the sacredness of contract, and destroyed the security of property – the two principles which constitute the essential distinction between a civilised and a savage state of society" ("Political Economy" 2). Philanthropy was condemned by, for instance, Trollope, James Anthony Froude, Whately, and Maine, who had famously stated that the movement of progressive societies was from status to contract. His great fear was that in Ireland the movement was in the opposite direction, with property and contract under relentless attack. Ireland needed "unflinching legislative surgery". We were, Maine wrote, "succumbing to a disease of modern origin which is enervating our fibre and softening our brain"; it was "really a deadly virus: *lues philanthropica*", which was "governing Ireland by Irish ideas". Legislation such as Gladstone's land Acts was killing Ireland with kindness, ensuring, according to Maine, the "survival of the unfittest" (qtd. in Ó Siocháin 75, 78, 76). Thomas Babington Macaulay defended masculine political economy against "blundering piety" or what he elsewhere denounced as "effeminate mawkish philanthropy", while his desired "extirpation" of the aboriginal Irish was frustrated by the "sentimental moral philosophy" spread by "philanthropists" (Sullivan 79, 436, 262). But benevolence, kindness, and philanthropy were versions of charity, to be given or withheld at pleasure, and not, like justice, obligatory.

CONCLUSION

It could be argued that the discourse of political economy itself, systematized by Adam Smith in his *Wealth of Nations* (1776), was first seriously challenged by the Great Irish Famine, which bore a large responsibility, though not immediately, for fundamental discursive changes in the discipline. The critique of political economy, and especially of laissez-faire, did not bear fruit until the end of the 1850s, when even its most orthodox defenders, such as Hancock, were submitting it to a searching moral critique, downgrading its scientific character in the name of morality. Its abstract and unhistorical nature came under increasing attack, and there was growing skepticism concerning the universality of a political economy generated out of English experiences and ideas. An increasing emphasis on the historical, the comparative, and the institutional, combined with a moral and political critique, seriously undermined the universalist pretensions of orthodox political economy.

By the end of the 1850s, the moral critique and process of historicizing culminated in the work of two notable Irish practitioners, Cliffe Leslie and John Kells Ingram, who became the leading proponents of the historical school in the English-speaking world. A new version of political economy, more suitable to Irish circumstances and ideas, was more hospitable to state intervention and small-scale agriculture, and tended to be opposed to the commodification of land, to contract, and to the sacrosanctity of the market. Eventually, with the influence of evolutionary ideas and the rise of comparative ethnology, Ireland was seen as closer to archaic than to modern commercial society, a position strengthened by the ideological extrapolations from the ongoing translation of *The Ancient Laws and Institutes of Ireland*, the Brehon laws. This indigenous legal system sprung from a society radically at odds with modernity and to which, according to all the authorities, the principles of political economy had absolutely no relevance at all.

RESPONSIBILITY: According to Adam Smith, "Wherever there is great property, there is great inequality. For one very rich man, there must be at least five hundred poor, and the affluence of the few supposes the indigence of the many" (297). Liberty was bought at the expense of equality, so paupers remained in full and undisturbed possession of their poverty. As smallholdings were consolidated, their tenants were scattered, as nomads, "broken men", condemned to be free, including the freedom to starve, a freedom widely exercised. But devotion to market fundamentalism was frequently condemned as idolatry. Bishop Hughes spoke of the "invisible but all-pervading divinity of the Fiscal, the unseen ruler of the temporal affairs of this world" (18). According to him, speaking of this fiscal force,

The premier of England is reported to have said not long since, "that nothing prevented him from employing government vessels to carry bread to a starving people, except his unwillingness to disturb the current of trade". Never was oracle of a hidden and a heartless deity uttered more faithfully, or more in accordance with the worship of its votaries, than in

Figure 14 | Unknown artist, *Servants of the Lord, Rendering an Account of their Stewardship During the Famine of 1847. Deaths by Starvation*

the language here imputed to the British minister, who may be fairly regarded as the living high priest of political economy (20).

Mitchel wrote of the "saving doctrines" of political economy as "the creed or gospel of England" (*History of Ireland* 210), while James Connolly held that "all except a few men had elevated landlord property and capitalist political economy to a fetish to be worshipped and upon the altar of that fetish Ireland perished" (110). In the view of many during the Great Famine, Mammon, the god of political economy **[Figure 14]**, demanded sacrifice, human sacrifice.

DEATH and POLITICAL ECONOMY: The relationship between political economy and death was put starkly by Benjamin Jowett: "I have always felt a certain horror of political economists ... since I heard one of them say that he feared the famine of 1848 in Ireland would not kill more than a million people, and that would scarcely be enough to do much good" (qtd. in Woodham-Smith 375–6). Bentinck told the House of Commons that the government knew of the people "dying in their thousands" by "their principles of free trade, yes, free trade in the lives of Irish people" (qtd. in Nally 5). Captain Thomas, a Cornish "miner", was scandalized to find that "in a Christian country, in a time of profound peace", people should be left to live or die "on political economy", while Rev. R. B. Townsend protested that "the principles of political economy have been carried out in practice to a murderous extent" (qtd. in Hickey 202–3).

Mitchel, in the most eloquent presentation of death by discourse, wrote of Ireland as dying unheroically of political economy:

If one should narrate how the cause of his country was stricken down in open battle, and blasted to pieces with shot and shell, there might be a certain mournful pride in dwelling upon the gallant resistance ... but to describe how the spirit of a country has been broken and subdued by beggarly famine ... how her life and soul have been ameliorated and civilized out of her; – how she died of political economy, and was buried under tons of official stationery; – this is a dreary task, which I wish some one else had undertaken (*Last Conquest of Ireland* 138–9).

One of the most acute commentators on the Famine, Bishop Hughes, in effect saw it as the consequence of sin, the sin of Adam, Adam Smith. Its cause was systemic and discursive, "the vice which is inherent in our system of social and political economy", so subtle that

it eludes all pursuit, that you cannot find or trace it to any responsible source. The man, indeed, over whose dead body the coroner holds the inquest, has been murdered, but no one has killed him. There is no external wound, there is no symptom of internal disease. Society guarded him against all outward violence; – it merely encircled him around in order to keep up what is termed the regular current of trade, and then political economy, with an invisible hand, applied the air pump to the narrow limits within which he was confined, and exhausted the atmosphere of his physical life. Who did it? No one did it, and yet it has been done (22).

The catastrophe was attributed to occult forces and unseen agencies, pre-eminent among them Smith's "hidden hand", with its central role in guarding, to use the words of Lady Wilde, "our masters' granaries from the thin hands of the poor" (10).

In a pervasive metaphor, Ireland was figured as a diseased body in need of the harsh medicine of political economy, the only balm in Gilead. Emigration, for example, was for some a life-threatening hemorrhage, for others the curative phlebotomy of a plethoric body. For Carlyle, society in Ireland was "collapsing in an orgy of autophagous self-annihilation" (McLean 95). In his words, "Society *here* would have to eat itself, and end by cannibalism in a week, if it were not held up by the rest of our empire still standing afoot" (qtd. in McLean 95) **[Figure 15]**. In obedience to the dictates of economy, people died of marasmus, a wasting away of the body. As a final act of obeisance, famine victims often became their own executioners, and, as Clarendon's "human potatoes", obligingly consumed themselves, potatophagi to the end, an act of autophagy that constituted an advance on Swift's *A Modest Proposal*. But death sometimes came as plenitude, by water (making Irish people more like their bogs), by edema, "famine dropsy", or hydropsy, a swelling of the body and limbs to several times their normal size, in grotesque mimicry of repletion. To further evade responsibility for death by Famine, even pain itself was sometimes denied. Trollope, for instance, claimed that though the Famine brought death, *in articulo mortis* it brought no pain: "There were no signs of acute agony … none of the horrid symptoms of gnawing hunger by which one generally supposes that famine is accompanied. The look is one of apathy, desolation, and death" (358). The Famine subjected the Irish poor to what Michael Watts calls "silent violence" and Rob Nixon "slow violence", killing them softly, discursively, and seemingly without human agency. The hidden hand was manifestly *lámh láidir*, in the Irish language literally a "strong hand" but actually meaning "violence". The starving Irish did not register an effective demand for food; wanting wants, they died of want. Not for them the cornucopia of classical antiquity or the cauldron of Dagda; instead they suffered the fate of Tantalus, and the Famine was for them a Barmecide feast.

The Famine was the forced march of the Irish people to the capitalist future, what Nally calls a "short cut to modernity" (64). Political economy outsourced morality to the market, so those who profited from this market fundamentalism and those who defended it had cases to answer. A million Irish people died for freedom: the freedom of the market. But there was no such thing as a free market: someone had to pay.

THE IRISH OGRE FATTENING ON THE FINEST PISANTRY.

Figure 15 | "The Irish Ogre Fattening on the Finest Pisantry [sic]" (*Punch*, vol. v, 1843)

ENDNOTES

[1] For further details on the defense of political economy, see Thomas A. Boylan and Timothy P. Foley, "'A nation perishing of political economy'?" in *"Fearful Realities": New Perspectives on the Famine*, eds Chris Morash and Richard Hayes (Dublin: Irish Academic Press, 1996), 138–50. For details on opposition to the discipline, see Thomas A. Boylan and Timothy P. Foley, "'The gospel of Mammon?' The Great Irish Famine and the critique of political economy", in *The Famine Lectures/Léachtaí an Ghorta*, ed. Breandán Ó Conaire (Boyle, County Roscommon: Comhdháil an Chraoibhín [1998?]), 152–65. For the ideological contexts of these debates, see Thomas A. Boylan and Timothy P. Foley, *Political Economy and Colonial Ireland: The Propagation and Ideological Function of Economic Discourse in the Nineteenth Century* (London and New York: Routledge, 1992).

[2] This is the illustrated jacket, by John Wallace, of a booklet produced by Cope's Tobacco Company of Liverpool in 1893 entitled *John Ruskin on Himself and Things in General*. It pictures Ruskin, astride a winged horse, slaying "political economy" still grasping a bag of money ("L.S.D.") on which is inscribed "Wealth of Nations", and with a volume entitled *The Dismal Science* fallen by his side.

WORKS CITED

Adair, A. Shafto. *The Winter of 1846–7 in Antrim: With Remarks on Out-door Relief and Colonization.* 3rd edn. London: James Ridgway, 1847.

Anon. *What Science Is Saying about Ireland*. Kingston-Upon-Hull: Leng, 1881.

Brady, Ciaran. *James Anthony Froude: An Intellectual Biography of a Victorian Prophet.* Oxford: Oxford University Press, 2013.

Burke, Edmund. *Thoughts and Details on Scarcity*. London: F. and C. Rivington, 1800.

Butt, Isaac. *A Voice for Ireland: The Famine in the Land: What Has Been Done and What Is to Be Done.* Dublin: James McGlashan, 1847.

Commissioners of National Education in Ireland. *Fifteenth Report of Commissioners of National Education in Ireland.* 1848.

Connolly, James. *Labour in Irish History*. 1910. Dublin: New Books, 1983.

Donnelly, Jr, James S. *The Great Irish Potato Famine*. Gloucestershire: Sutton, 2001.

Fitzpatrick, W. J. *Memoirs of Richard Whately: Archbishop of Dublin: With a Glance at His Contemporaries and Times.* Vol. 2 (2 vols). London: Bentley, 1864.

Gibbons, Luke. "Peripheral modernities: national and global in a post-colonial frame". *Nineteenth-century Contexts*, 29.2–3 (June/September 2007): 271–81.

Gray, Peter. "British public opinion and the Great Irish Famine, 1845–49". *The Famine Lectures/ Léachtaí an Ghorta*. Ed. Breandán Ó Conaire. Boyle, County Roscommon: Comhdháil an Chraoibhín, 1995–97: 77–106.

---. *Famine, Land and Politics: British Government and Irish Society, 1843–1850.* Dublin and Portland, OR: Irish Academic Press, 1999.

Hall, John. *Irish Character: A Lecture Delivered Before the Young Men's Christian Association, at Exeter Hall, December 4, 1866.* London: J. Nisbet [1866?].

Hancock, William Neilson. *Three Lectures on the Questions: Should the Principles of Political Economy Be Disregarded at the Present Crisis?* .... Dublin: Hodges and Smith, 1847.

---. "A notice of the theory 'that there is no hope for a nation which lives on potatoes'". *Transactions of the Dublin Statistical Society* 1 (April 1848).

---. "On the economic causes of the present state of agriculture in Ireland: part ii: legal impediments to the transfer of land". *Transactions of the Dublin Statistical Society* 1 (December 1848).

---. "Economic views of Bishop Berkeley and Mr. Butt with respect to the theory 'that a nation may gain by the compulsory use of native manufactures'". *Transactions of the Dublin Statistical Society* 1 (May 1849).

---. "On the bothy system of lodging farm labourers in Scotland ...". *Journal of the Dublin Statistical Society* 2 (January 1860).

---. "Remittances from North America by Irish emigrants ...". *Journal of the Statistical and Social Enquiry Society of Ireland* 4 (1873).

Hearn, W. E. *The Cassell Prize Essay on the Condition of Ireland*. London: Cassell, 1851.

---. *Plutology: Or the Theory of the Efforts to Satisfy Human Wants.* Melbourne: George Robertson, 1863.

---. *The Aryan Household: Its Structure and Its Development* .... Melbourne: George Robertson, 1878.

Hickey, Patrick. "The Famine in the Skibbereen Union (1845–51)". *The Great Irish Famine.* Ed. Cathal Póirtéir. Cork and Dublin: Mercier Press, 1995: 185–203.

Hughes, John. *A Lecture on the Antecedent Causes of the Irish Famine in 1847*. New York: Edward Dunigan, 1847.

"An Irish Liberal". *Irish Issues*. Dublin: E. Ponsonby, 1886.

Kinealy, Christine. *This Great Calamity: The Irish Famine 1845–52*. Dublin: Gill & Macmillan, 1994.

---. *A Death-dealing Famine: The Great Hunger in Ireland*. London and Chicago: Pluto Press, 1997.

---. *The Great Irish Famine: Impact, Ideology and Rebellion*. Basingstoke and New York: Palgrave, 2002.

Lawson, James Anthony. *Five Lectures on Political Economy: Delivered Before the University of Dublin, in Michaelmas Term, 1843*. London: John W. Parker, 1844.

Lewis, George Cornwall. *Local Disturbances in Ireland; and on the Irish Church Question*. London: B. Fellowes, 1836.

Lloyd, David. "The indigent sublime: specters of Irish hunger". *Representations*, 92, 1 (fall 2005): 152–85.

Longfield, Mountifort. *Four Lectures on Poor Laws*. Dublin: William Curry, 1834.

McLean, Stuart. *The Event and Its Terrors: Ireland, Famine, Modernity*. Stanford, CA: Stanford University Press, 2004.

Mill, John Stuart. *Principles of Political Economy: With Some of Their Applications to Social Philosophy*. Ed. J. M. Robson. *Collected Works*. Vol. 3 (33 vols). London: Routledge, 1965.

Mitchel, John. *The History of Ireland*. Vol. 2 (2 vols). Glasgow and London: Cameron and Ferguson, n.d.

---. *The Last Conquest of Ireland (Perhaps)*. Glasgow: R. & T. Washbourne, 1861.

Morash, Christopher. *Writing the Irish Famine*. Oxford: Clarendon Press, 1995.

Nally, David P. *Human Encumbrances: Political Violence and the Great Irish Famine*. Notre Dame, IN: University of Notre Dame Press, 2011.

Newman, John Henry [Cardinal]. *The Idea of a University*. London: Longmans, Green, 1886.

O'Rourke, J. *The History of the Great Irish Famine of 1847*. 2nd edn. London and Dublin: McGlashan & Gill, Duffy, 1874.

Ó Síocháin, Séamas. "Sir Henry Maine and the survival of the fittest". Ed. Séamas Ó Síocháin. *Social Thought on Ireland in the Nineteenth Century*. Dublin: University College Dublin Press, 2009: 67–96.

"Political Economy". *The Irish Landlord and His Accusers: With an Account of Misguided Legislation and Consequent Demoralization and Danger, Social and Political*. Dublin: Hodges, Figgis, 1882.

Richey, A. G. *A Short History of the Irish People* ... Dublin: Hodges, Figgis, 1887.

Senior, William Nassau. *Journals, Conversations and Essays Relating to Ireland*. Vol. 1 (2 vols). London: Longmans, Green, 1868.

Shackleton, Ebenezer. "Thoughts on reading the Hon. John P. Vereker's paper on absenteeism", *Transactions of the Dublin Statistical Society* 2 (1849–51).

Smith, Adam. *An Inquiry into the Nature and Causes of the Wealth of Nations*. London: Thomas Nelson, 1850.

Somerville, Alexander. *Letters from Ireland During the Famine of 1847*. Ed. K. D. M. Snell. Dublin: Irish Academic Press, 1994.

Sullivan, Robert E. *Macaulay: The Tragedy of Power*. Cambridge, MA: Harvard University Press, 2009.

Torrens, R. *Self Supporting Colonization: Ireland Saved, Without Cost to the Imperial Treasury*. London: James Ridgway & Smith, Elder, 1847.

Trevelyan, C. E. *The Irish Crisis*. London: Longman, Brown, Green & Longmans, 1848.

Trollope, Anthony. *Castle Richmond*. 1860. London: Trollope Society, 1994.

"An Ulsterman" [George Sigerson]. *Modern Ireland: Its Vital Questions, Secret Societies, and Government*. London: Longmans, Green, Reader & Dyer, 1868.

Whately, Richard. *Introductory Lectures on Political Economy*. 3rd edn. London: John W. Parker, 1847.

---. "Report of the address on the conclusion of the first session of the Dublin Statistical Society". *Transactions of the Dublin Statistical Society* 1 (June 1848).

[---]. *Easy Lessons on Money Matters: For the Use of Young People*. 13th edn. London: John W. Parker, 1853.

Whelan, Kevin. "Clachans: landscape and life in Ireland before and after the Famine". *At the Anvil: Essays in Honour of William J. Smyth*. Eds. Patrick J. Duffy and William Nolan. Dublin: Geography Publications, 2012: 453–75.

Wilde, Lady ("Speranza"). "The Famine Year". *Poems*. 2nd edn. Glasgow and London: Cameron & Ferguson, n.d.

Woodham-Smith, Cecil. *The Great Hunger: Ireland 1845–1849*. 1962. London: Hamish Hamilton, 1987.

IMAGES

Cover
Micheal Farrell
1940–2000
Portrait of Charles Trevelyan
1997–98
Mixed media on canvas
19.7 x 15.7 in (50 x 39.9 cm)
© Estate of Micheal Farrell
Image provided by Ireland's
Great Hunger Museum,
Quinnipiac University

Figure 1
"The Absentee. Scene Naples.
Enter the Ghosts of Starv'd
Irish Peasentry [*sic*]!!!"
Looking Glass
No. 8, August 1, 1830
National Library of Ireland

Figure 2
John Wallace
Cover of John Ruskin, *John
Ruskin on Himself and Things
in General*
Liverpool: Office of Cope's
Tobacco Plant, 1893

Figure 3
Eden Upton Eddis
1812–1901
*Sir Charles Edward Trevelyan,
1st Bt (1890-1886)* [Detail]
1850
Oil on canvas
95 x 59.1 in (241.5 x 150 cm)
© National Trust Images

Figure 4
Richard Whately
Images from title pages of *Easy
Lessons on Money Matters: For
the Use of Young People*
13th edn. London: John W.
Parker, 1853

Figure 5
Eden Upton Eddis
1812–1901
*Sir Charles Edward Trevelyan,
1st Bt (1809–1886)*
1850
Oil on canvas
95 x 59.1 in (241.5 x 150 cm)
© National Trust Images

Figure 6
"Peel's Panacea for Ireland"
Punch
Vol. xvi, 1849
Image provided by Ireland's
Great Hunger Museum,
Quinnipiac University

Figure 7
William Elmes
fl. 1797-1815
Irish Bogtrotters
c. 1812
Hand-colored etching
9.8 x 13.7 in (25 x 34.7 cm)
© The Trustees of the British
Museum

Figure 8
"The New Irish Still"
Punch
Vol. xvii, 1849
Image provided by Ireland's
Great Hunger Museum,
Quinnipiac University

Figure 9
"The Settlement on Achile [*sic*]
Island"
Pictorial Times
November 7, 1846
Image provided by Ireland's
Great Hunger Museum,
Quinnipiac University

Figure 10
"The Real Potato Blight of
Ireland (from a Sketch Taken in
Conciliation Hall)"
Punch
Vol. ix, 1845
Image provided by Ireland's
Great Hunger Museum,
Quinnipiac University

Figure 11
Henry Heath (Paul Pry)
1794–1840
A Sketch of the Great Agi-tater
1829
Hand-colored etching
14.3 x 10.5 in (36.4 x 26.7 cm)
© The Trustees of the British
Museum

Figure 12
"Gog and Magog Giving Paddy
a Lift Out of the Mire"
Punch
Vol. xvii, 1849
Image provided by Ireland's
Great Hunger Museum,
Quinnipiac University

Figure 13
"Here and There; or Emigration
a Remedy"
Punch
Vol. xv, 1848
Image provided by Ireland's
Great Hunger Museum,
Quinnipiac University

Figure 14
Unknown artist
*Servants of the Lord, Rendering
an Account of their Stewardship
During the Famine of 1847.
Deaths by Starvation*
1847
Lithograph
9.4 x 12.3 in (24 x 31.2 cm)
© The Trustees of the British
Museum

Figure 15
"The Irish Ogre Fattening on
the Finest Pisantry [*sic*]"
Punch
Vol. v, 1843
Image provided by Ireland's
Great Hunger Museum,
Quinnipiac University

ABOUT THE AUTHOR

Tadhg Foley, a native of Donoughmore, County Cork, is professor emeritus of English at the National University of Ireland, Galway. He was educated at Galway and Merton College, Oxford; he has been a Fulbright scholar-in-residence at the University of San Francisco, has held the O'Donnell Fellowship at the University of Melbourne, and has served as visiting professor, Study of Religions Department, University College, Cork. He has published extensively in nineteenth-century Irish studies, with (in collaboration with Professor Tom Boylan) a special emphasis on Irish political economy and its ideological role. Their *Political Economy and Colonial Ireland* was published in 1992; they later edited a four-volume anthology, *Irish Political Economy* (2003), and, in six volumes, *John Elliot Cairnes: Collected Works* (2004).

IRELAND'S GREAT HUNGER MUSEUM | QUINNIPIAC UNIVERSITY PRESS ©2016

SERIES EDITORS

Niamh O'Sullivan
Grace Brady

IMAGE RESEARCH

Claire Puzarne

DESIGN

Rachel Foley

ACKNOWLEDGMENT

Office of Public Affairs, Quinnipiac University

PUBLISHER

Quinnipiac University Press

PRINTING

GRAPHYCEMS

ISBN 978-0-9978374-1-4

Ireland's Great Hunger Museum
Quinnipiac University

3011 Whitney Avenue
Hamden, CT 06518-1908
203-582-6500

www.ighm.org